Guided Reading Notes

Dark Blue Band
Oxford Level 16

Hidden Depths

Contents

OXFORD
UNIVERSITY PRESS

Introduction

Why is guided reading important?

Guided reading plays an important role in your whole-school provision for reading, providing opportunities for children to progress and develop the key competencies they need to become confident and skilled independent readers. Working with small groups of children, with texts closely matched to the readers' needs, guided reading is the perfect vehicle for delivering focused teaching from Reception/P1 right through to Year 6/P7. The teacher-pupil interaction also provides a valuable assessment opportunity, helping you identify exactly what each child can and can't do. Through guided reading children also encounter a world of exciting, whole books – building a community of readers who read for pleasure.

About *Project X Origins*

Project X Origins is a comprehensive, whole-school guided reading programme designed to help you teach the wide range of skills essential to ensure children progress as readers and to help nurture a love of reading.

Ensuring the key skills are covered

Project X Origins incorporates all of the key skills children need to develop to become successful and enthusiastic readers:

- **Word reading:** phonically regular and common exception words are introduced systematically in the early levels with phonic opportunities provided throughout the notes. As children progress, they are encouraged to use their decoding skills whenever they encounter new or unfamiliar words, and also to recognize how this impacts on different spelling rules.

- **Comprehension:** understanding what has been read is central to being an effective and engaged reader but comprehension is not something that comes automatically so specific strategies have been built into the notes to ensure children develop comprehension skills they can use over a range of texts:
  - Previewing
  - Predicting
  - Activating and building prior knowledge
  - Questioning
  - Recalling
  - Visualizing and other sensory responses
  - Deducting, inferring and drawing conclusions
  - Determining importance
  - Synthesizing
  - Empathizing
  - Summarizing
  - Personal response, including adopting a critical response
- **Reading fluency:** fluency occurs as children develop automatic word recognition, reading with pace and expression. Strategies to help achieve this, including meaningful opportunities for oral reading, re-reading and re-listening are provided throughout.
- **Vocabulary:** introducing new vocabulary within a meaningful context is an important element in extending children's vocabulary range, developing their reading fluency and comprehension. Each thematic cluster provides opportunities for revisiting and reinforcing vocabulary over a range of books and contexts.
- **Grammar, punctuation and spelling:** learning about language in the context of a text, rather than through a series of discrete exercises, can help make grammar, punctuation and spelling relevant and helps children make the link between grammar, punctuation and clarity of meaning, thus supporting their development as writers. Opportunities to support an in-depth look at language are provided for every book from Year 1/P2 to Year 6/P7.
- **Spoken language:** talk is crucial to learning and developing their comprehension so children are given plenty of opportunities to: discuss and debate their ideas with others; justify their opinions; ask and answer questions; explore and hypothesise; summarise, describe and explain; and listen and respond to the ideas of others.

Assessment and progression in reading

Project X Origins includes a rigorous assessment spine drawn from the *Oxford Ros Wilson Reading Criterion Scale* to ensure that you know exactly what each child can do and what they need to focus on next in order to make progress. This assessment framework, combined with the careful levelling of the Oxford Levels, will help you select the right book with the right level of challenge for each of your guided reading groups and to assess, track and monitor each child's progress.

Step 1

On a termly basis, use the *Reading Criterion Scale* (which can be found in the relevant *Project X Origins Teaching Handbook*) to assess each child's reading. The scale will tell you the Oxford Level a child is comfortable reading at, and the areas a child needs to develop. You can also use this assessment to form your guided reading groups.

Step 2

Plan your guided reading sessions by selecting books at the appropriate Oxford Level that focus on the relevant learning needs of the group. You will find charts showing the learning objectives and assessment points for every *Project X Origins* book in the relevant *Project X Origins Teaching Handbook*. Depending on your assessment, you might choose a book at the level the children are comfortable at or one from the next level up, to offer some stretch.

Step 3

Use the assessment points within the Guided Reading Notes to support on-going assessment of children's reading progress. The Progress Tracking Charts in the relevant *Project X Origins Teaching Handbook* can be used to record this if you wish. Regularly re-assess each child's progress combining your on-going informal assessments and the termly assessment using the *Reading Criterion Scale*. Use this information to re-organize guided reading groups and teaching plans in response to children's varying degrees of progress.

Getting started: using the Guided Reading Notes

At a glance

Project X Origins Guided Reading Notes offer detailed guidance to help deliver effective and engaging guided reading sessions, and are designed to be used flexibly to ensure you get the most out of each book. For notes containing multiple sessions, you may choose to focus on each of these sessions or focus on one session and have the children read the rest of the book independently.

Curricula correlation and assessment

At the beginning of every set of notes there are correlation charts for all UK curricula, ensuring that across the clusters the main curricula objectives are covered. In addition, an overview of assessment points for each book is provided – these points are also signposted throughout the notes.

Key information

Before the first session, an overview of the book and the resources you will need (such as additional photocopy masters) is provided.

Teaching sequence

Each guided reading session follows the same teaching sequence:

- **Before reading**: children explore the context of each book to support their understanding and help them engage with the text. They are encouraged to discuss, recall, respond, predict and speculate about the book. Opportunities to focus on word reading and/or vocabulary are also introduced at this point.
- **During reading**: children are given a section of the book to read with specific questions in mind.
- **After reading**: children reflect on and discuss what they have read. They are encouraged to delve deeper, exploring their understanding of the text, developing their vocabulary, grammar, punctuation, spelling and fluency where appropriate.
- **Follow-up**: opportunities for children to extend their learning outside the session are provided, including writing and cross-curricular activities.

Throughout the sessions, the key strategies that children are developing are clearly identified.

Operation Shipwreck

BY ANTHONY McGOWAN

Curricula correlation

English National Curriculum

Spoken language	Participate in discussions and debates
Word reading	Apply their growing knowledge of root words, prefixes and suffixes (morphology and etymology), both to read aloud and to understand the meaning of new words that they meet
Comprehension	Predict what might happen from details stated and implied
	Discuss and evaluate how authors use language, including figurative language, considering the impact on the reader
	Draw inferences and justify these with evidence from the text

Developing grammar, punctuation, vocabulary and spelling

Grammar and Punctuation	Relative clauses beginning with *who, which, where, why, whose, that*	… moaned Ant, who looked as green as their craft. … she beamed the data to the Green Dart's on-board computer, which showed them on a map …
	Linking ideas across paragraphs using adverbials of time	By that time
Vocabulary and Spelling	Challenge and context words	Mediterranean, desperately, shrunken, refuges, analysing, endangered, inquisitive, stabilize, spiralled, aquatic, mechanical

Reading assessment points

Word reading	Can the children read a range of level appropriate texts fluently and accurately?
Comprehension	Can the children infer and deduce meaning based on evidence drawn from different points in the text?
	Can the children discuss messages, moods, feelings and attitudes using the clues from the text using inference and deduction skills?
	Can the children quote directly from the text to answer questions?
	Can the children read between the lines, using clues from action, dialogue and description to interpret meaning and/or explain what characters are thinking/feeling and the way they act?
	Can the children discuss how an author builds a character through dialogue, action, description?
	Can the children identify the ways in which paragraphs are linked?
	Can the children compare the structure of different stories to discover how they differ in pace, build-up, sequence, complication and resolution?
	Can the children skim and scan to identify key ideas in the text?

Scottish Curriculum for Excellence

Listening and talking	When listening and talking with others for different purposes, I can: share information, experiences and opinions; identify issues raised and summarise main points or findings; clarify points by asking questions or by asking others to say more LIT 2-09a
Reading	I can select and use a range of strategies and resources before I read, and as I read, to make meaning clear and give reasons for my selection LIT 2-13a
	I regularly select and read, listen to or watch texts which I enjoy and find interesting, and I can explain why I prefer certain texts and authors LIT 2-11a
	I can discuss the writer's style and other features appropriate to genre ENG 2-19a
	Through developing my knowledge of context clues, punctuation, grammar and layout, I can read unfamiliar texts with increasing fluency, understanding and expression ENG 2-12a

Welsh National Literacy Framework

Oracy	Explain information and ideas, exploring and using ways to be convincing, e.g. use of vocabulary, gesture, visual aids
Reading	Contribute to group discussion, taking some responsibility for completing the task well, e.g. introducing relevant ideas, summing up (Collaboration)
	Use a range of strategies to make meaning from words and sentences, including knowledge of phonics, word roots, word families, syntax, text organisation and prior knowledge of context (Reading strategies)
	Read complex texts independently for sustained periods (Reading strategies)
	Identify and explore ideas and information that interest them (Comprehension)
	Infer meaning which is not explicitly stated, e.g. what happens next?, why did he/she do that? (Comprehension)

Northern Ireland Curriculum

Talking and Listening	Share, respond to and evaluate ideas, arguments and points of view and use evidence or reason to justify opinions, actions or proposals
Reading	Use a range of cross-checking strategies to read unfamiliar words in texts
	Consider, interpret and discuss texts, exploring the ways in which language can be manipulated in order to affect the reader or engage attention

Session 1 (Chapters 1–3)

About this book

Team X meet their old adversary the Collector again. He has sent his evil Master-bot to the Aegean Sea to steal the wreck of a sunken treasure ship. The ecosystem is in danger … can Team X stop him?

You will need

- *Prediction and reflection grid* Photocopy Master, *Teaching Handbook* for Year 5/P6
- *Expedition* Photocopy Master, *Teaching Handbook* for Year 5/P6

Before reading

- Discuss the title *Operation Shipwreck*. Which type of organizations call their investigations and activities 'operations'? **(activating prior knowledge)**
- Look at the map on pages 4 and 5. Can the children locate the UK and other countries in Europe, and the Mediterranean Sea/ Atlantic and Pacific Oceans? Can they link any current news stories to any place discussed? **(activating prior knowledge)**
- Read pages 2 and 3 to the children. Model fluent reading through the pace and expression of your reading. **(developing fluency, engaging readers)**
- Working in pairs, ask the children to predict what sort of 'mischief and mayhem' the Collector might do in this book. They could use the *Prediction and reflection grid* Photocopy Master to record their thoughts. **(predicting)**
- Remind the children what to do if they encounter a difficult word, or if they struggle to understand the meaning of a word or a sentence.

During reading

- Ask the children to read Chapters 1–3.
- As they read, ask them to spot how page 13 has been designed to reflect the non-fiction text type.

Assessment point

Can the children infer and deduce meaning based on evidence drawn from different points in the text?

Can the children discuss messages, moods, feelings and attitudes using the clues from the text using inference and deduction skills?

After reading

Returning to the text

Ask the children:

- Where does the story take place? **(recall)**
- Why was the Collector gazing thoughtfully at his globes? **(deducing, inferring)**
- Why is the monk seal in danger? **(drawing conclusions, synthesizing)**
- Before session 2, ask the children to read Chapters 2–4 independently.

Assessment point

Can the children quote directly from the text to answer questions?

The author's craft

- Discuss why the last two lines of Chapter 1 are so effective and ask why the author has used italics for *now*.
- Why has the author written such a short Chapter 3?

Developing comprehension

- During a short guided writing session, demonstrate how to change the beginning of Chapter 2 from narrative into play script. Ask the children to work in pairs to complete the script of the chapter.
- The children can then perform the scene from their script, using gestures to reflect how the characters are feeling.

- Prior to Session 2, ensure the children have read Chapter 4 independently.

Session 2 (Chapter 5)

Before reading

- Ask the children to briefly recap the story to date. **(recall)**
- How might the Green Dart help the characters to stop the Master-bot from turning the wreck into a snow globe? Ask the children to fill in their *Prediction and reflection grid* Photocopy Master. **(predicting)**

During reading

- Ask the children to read Chapter 5.
- As they read, ask them to think about how each member of Team X reacts to the situation.

Assessment point
Can the children read a range of level appropriate texts fluently and accurately?

After reading

Returning to the text

Ask the children:

- What was stirring up the sediment on the sea floor? **(recall, inferring)**
- Why did Tiger grin on page 30? **(inferring)**
- Ant begins to 'fiddle' with the control panel on page 31. What does that tell the reader about his capabilities? **(inferring)**
- How did each character react during the battle with the X-bots? Use evidence from the text. **(inferring, drawing conclusions, synthesizing)**

Assessment point
Can the children read between the lines, using clues from action, dialogue and description to interpret meaning and/or explain what characters are thinking/ feeling and the way they act?

The author's craft

- Tiger says "*Uh, oh*" on page 28 when he is faced with all the X5 guards. Ask the children to discuss with a partner why the author has deliberately chosen such an understated phrase. What does this tell them about Tiger? **(adopting a critical stance, inferring)**
- On page 31, the author shows the reader how Max and Tiger were feeling without telling us that they were frightened (e.g. *heart hammered*). Ask the children to discuss this with their partner and then write how Ant and Cat might be feeling at this point, using similar techniques.

Assessment point
Can the children discuss how an author builds a character through dialogue, action, description?

Developing grammar, punctuation and spelling

- Ask the children to look at the clause *who looked as green as ...* on page 22. Explain that this is a relative clause which gives additional information about the first clause and is connected to the main clause by a word such as *that, which, who, whom* or *whose*. Can they find any other relative clauses in the chapters they have just read? Discuss when each word should be used, e.g. *who/whom* when referring to people.

- Prior to Session 3, ensure the children have read Chapter 6 independently.

Session 3 (Chapters 7–8)

Before reading

- Ask the children to predict what will happen in the rest of the story. **(personal response, predicting)**

During reading

- Ask the children to read Chapters 7–8.
- As they read, ask them to reflect on their response to the whole story. **(personal response)**

After reading

Returning to the text

- In pairs, ask the children to discuss what they thought of the story. They could also complete their *Prediction and reflection grid* Photocopy Master if they started one. **(personal response, adopting a critical stance)**

The author's craft

- How does the author build excitement in the last chapter? How do the illustrations help the reader? **(deducing, inferring, determining importance, adopting a critical stance)**

Assessment point

Can the children compare the structure of different stories to discover how they differ in pace, build-up, sequence, complication and resolution?

Developing comprehension

- Ask the children to complete a storyboard, summarizing the final chapter in 12 frames. **(visualizing, summarizing, determining importance)**
- Ask them to use this to turn a chapter into a play script, drawing on the conventions of play script explored in Session 1.

Assessment point
Can the children skim and scan to identify key ideas in the text?

Developing grammar, punctuation and spelling

- Discuss how the author conveys the passage of time across paragraphs. Look at examples of adverbials of time, e.g. *By that time*, and how they make links between paragraphs. Explain that many of these examples are fronted adverbials (they appear at the start of the sentence). Discuss how fronted adverbials are always followed by a comma.

Assessment point
Can the children identify the ways in which paragraphs are linked?

Follow-up

Writing activities

- Choose one member of Team X and write a character profile, using the one on page 3 as a model. **(short writing task)**
- Use the *Expedition* Photocopy Master to advertise a visit to a Mediterranean shipwreck. **(short writing task)**
- Write a confidential email explaining how Team X was able to stop the Collector this time. **(longer writing task)**

Cross-curricular activities

- Look at underwater images in Google Earth to find out what the sea really looks like. **(Geography, Computing)**
- Design a snow globe using Photoshop. **(DT)**
- Compose an underwater musical scene with parts representing the tranquillity of the water, the fish, the wreck, the turtle (p.24) as Team X arrived. Use graphic notation to record the composition and perform it. **(Music)**

Toxic!

BY JAN BURCHETT AND SARA VOGLER

Curricula correlation

English National Curriculum

Spoken language	Use spoken language to develop understanding through speculating, hypothesising, imagining and exploring ideas
Word reading	Apply their growing knowledge of root words, prefixes and suffixes (morphology and etymology), both to read aloud and to understand the meaning of new words that they meet
Comprehension	Summarise the main ideas drawn from more than one paragraph, identifying key details that support the main ideas
	Discuss and evaluate how authors use language, including figurative language, considering the impact on the reader
	Provide reasoned justifications for their views

Developing grammar, punctuation, vocabulary and spelling

Grammar and Punctuation	Converting nouns into verbs using the suffixes *-ate* and *-ify*	activate, solidify
Vocabulary and Spelling	Words ending in *-able* and *-ible*	capable, horrible, terrible, responsible
	Challenge and context words	irritated, blackened, reluctantly, shimmered, slunk, furiously, eerie, crumpled, manoeuvred, accelerate, shuffling, tentacles, aggressively

Reading assessment points

Word reading	Can the children read a range of level appropriate texts fluently and accurately?
Comprehension	Can the children read between the lines, using clues from action, dialogue and description to interpret meaning and/or explain what characters are thinking/feeling and the way they act?
	Can the children talk about the effects of different words and phrases to create different images and atmosphere?
	Can the children identify relationships between characters, explaining the effects this has on the reader?
	Can the children refer to the text to support opinions and predictions?
	Can the children quote directly from the text to answer questions?
	Can the children discuss how an author builds character through dialogue, action, description?
	Can the children talk with friends about books and listen to others, in order to share book recommendations and widen understanding of the world?
	Can the children skim and scan to identify key ideas in the text?

Scottish Curriculum for Excellence

Listening and talking	I can recognise how the features of spoken language can help in communication, and I can use what I learn ENG 2-03a
Reading	I can select and use a range of strategies and resources before I read, and as I read, to make meaning clear and give reasons for my selection LIT 2-13a
	To show my understanding across different areas of learning, I can identify and consider the purpose and main ideas of a text and use supporting detail LIT 2-16a
	I can discuss the writer's style and other features appropriate to genre ENG 2-19a
	To help me develop an informed view, I can identify and explain the difference between fact and opinion, recognise when I am being influenced, and have assessed how useful and believable my sources are LIT 2-18a

Welsh National Literacy Framework

Oracy	Explore issues and themes through role play (Speaking)
Reading	Use a range of strategies to make meaning from words and sentences, including knowledge of phonics, word roots, word families, syntax, text organisation and prior knowledge of context (Reading strategies)
	Infer meaning which is not explicitly stated, e.g. what happens next?, why did he/she do that? (Comprehension)
	Identify and explore ideas and information that interest them (Comprehension)
	Gather and organise information and ideas from different sources (Response and analysis)

Northern Ireland Curriculum

Talking and Listening	Formulate, give and respond to guidance, directions and instructions
Reading	Use a range of cross-checking strategies to read unfamiliar words in texts
	Justify their responses logically, by inference, deduction and/or reference to evidence within the text, for example, compare and contrast two characters in a story or history text

Session 1 (Chapters 1–2)

About this book

Team X is sent to investigate what is causing the death of a beautiful area of Canadian forest. What they find is astonishing.

You will need

- Globe, atlases
- *Canadian National Parks* Photocopy Master, *Teaching Handbook* for Year 5/P6
- *Vocabulary bookmark* Photocopy Master, *Teaching Handbook* for Year 5/P6
- *What are they thinking, feeling, saying?* Photocopy Master, *Teaching Handbook* for Year 5/P6
- *NICE 'Mission Accomplished' report* Photocopy Master, *Teaching Handbook* for Year 5/P6

Before reading

- Look at pages 2–5 together. Check that the children understand the aim of NICE (protection of the planet and the precious things in it). **(activating prior knowledge)**
- Using atlases or a globe, locate Canada and Cape Breton. You could also refer to the *Canadian National Parks* Photocopy Master. **(activating prior knowledge)**

During reading

- Ask the children to read Chapters 1 and 2.
- As they read, ask them to note any new or unusual words and record these on their *Vocabulary bookmark* Photocopy Master.
- Ask the children to look out for words ending *-able* or *-ible*.

Assessment point

Can the children read a range of level appropriate texts fluently and accurately?

After reading

Returning to the text

Ask the children:

- In her blog, what does Mandy say she has found? **(recall)**
- Why was Tiger late for the meeting? **(recall)**
- Why did Dani warn the team that what they might find could be nasty? **(inferring)**
- Why is Tiger so negative? **(empathizing, inferring and drawing conclusions)**

Assessment point

Can the children read between the lines, using clues from action, dialogue and description to interpret meaning and/or explain what characters are thinking/feeling and the way they act?

The author's craft

- Look at the last three paragraphs on page 15. Identify all the words and phrases that bring the action to life. **(adopting a critical stance)**

Assessment point
Can the children talk about the effects of different words and phrases to create different images and atmosphere?

Developing comprehension

- Ask the children to role play the scene on page 12 and freeze frame where Cat gazes round at the devastation of the forest. Ask each character what they are thinking and feeling at this point. How could they persuade Tiger that something needs to be done? **(empathizing, personal response, adopting a critical stance)**
- Ask the children to complete the *What are they thinking, feeling, saying?* Photocopy Master for one of the characters. **(empathizing, adopting a critical stance)**

Assessment point
Can the children identify relationships between characters, explaining the effects this has on the reader?

Developing vocabulary

- Ask the children to highlight all the ecological vocabulary they noted on their bookmarks.

Developing grammar, punctuation and spelling

- Write the words *capable* and *horrible* on the board. Point out that the endings of the words are spelt differently even though they sound the same. Can they think of any other words ending in *-able* or *-ible*?

- Prior to session 2, ensure the children have read Chapter 3 independently.

Session 2 (Chapter 4)

Before reading

- Ask the children to recap briefly the story to date. **(recall)**
- Look at page 23, and ask them to predict what sort of creature might be in the tunnel. **(predicting)**

Assessment point
Can the children refer to the text to support opinions and predictions?

During reading

- Ask the children to read Chapter 4.
- As they read, ask them to notice the different functions of the Driller.
- Ask them to note any new or unusual words and record them on their bookmarks, e.g. *monstrous, contours*.

Assessment point
Can the children read a range of level appropriate texts fluently and accurately?

After reading

Returning to the text

Ask the children:

- What was the animal? What is its most distinguishing feature and what is it used for? **(recall)**
- What was wrong with the animal and how had this happened? **(recall, deducing, inferring, drawing conclusions)**
- What does a skull and crossbones usually represent? What does this make the reader think? **(activating prior knowledge, inferring)**

Assessment point
Can the children quote directly from the text to answer questions?

The author's craft

- Challenge the children to find all the hints the vocabulary gives as to what the creature might be, i.e. something not alien (e.g. *pawed*). **(inferring, deducing, drawing conclusions)**
- How is the tension created at the end of Chapter 4? How could children use this technique in their own writing? **(adopting a critical stance)**

Assessment point
Can the children talk about the effects of different words and phrases to create different images and atmosphere?

Developing vocabulary

- Share the words the children recorded on their bookmarks. Look at them in context and check they understand their meanings.
- Focus on the words with tricky spellings, e.g. *contours, reverberated, monstrous, metallic, manoeuvred* and *accelerated.* Ask the children to work out ways of remembering the spellings, e.g. using mnemonics or acrostics.

Developing grammar, punctuation and spelling

- Write the word *active* on the board. Ask the children what kind of word this is. (A noun) Can they suggest how this word could be turned into a verb? Demonstrate adding *-ate* to the end to form the verb *activate*. What other verbs have been formed in this way in this book? (*identify*) Could they try applying this to other nouns?

- Prior to Session 3, ensure the children have read Chapters 5–6 independently.

Session 3 (Chapters 7–8)

Before reading

- Ask the children to discuss the story so far. How do the authors make the adventure exciting? **(recall, personal response, adopting a critical stance)**
- What do they predict will happen next? **(predicting)**
- Read pages 45–48 aloud. Model the excitement and tension in the prose and the different voices for each character and their feelings. Ask the children which techniques you used to bring the story to life. **(engaging readers, developing fluency)**

Assessment point
Can the children discuss how an author builds a character through dialogue, action, description?

During reading

- Ask the children to read Chapters 7 and 8.
- As they read, ask them to look out for independent clauses.
- As they read, ask them to reflect on their response to the whole story. **(personal response)**

After reading

Returning to the text

- In pairs, ask the children to discuss what they thought of the story. Which bits did they particularly like or dislike? **(personal response, adopting a critical stance)**

> **Assessment point**
> Can the children talk with friends about books and listen to others, in order to share book recommendations and widen understanding of the world?

Developing comprehension

- Ask the children to complete a storyboard, summarizing the whole story in 12 frames. **(visualizing, summarizing, determining importance)**

> **Assessment point**
> Can the children skim and scan to identify key ideas in the text?

- Ask them to skim the book, highlighting examples of Tiger's character through his reactions, then write the story from his point of view.

> **Assessment point**
> Can the children discuss how an author builds a character through dialogue, action, description?

Follow-up

Writing activities

- Reread page 39 and write a poem about being in this dramatic situation. **(short writing task)**
- Write Twitter entries throughout the day (maximum of 140 characters per entry). **(short writing task)**
- Write the end-of-mission report that Dani will file in NICE's records on the *NICE 'Mission Accomplished' report* Photocopy Master. **(longer writing task)**

Cross-curricular activities

- Use a variety of software to devise a multimedia storyboard to create an animated version of the action. **(Computing)**
- Research Cape Breton and other parks in Canada using the *Canadian National Parks* Photocopy Master. **(Geography)**
- Use a digital camera to produce a TV advert to persuade people to visit Cape Breton. **(Computing)**

Journey to the Centre of the Earth

BY PAUL SHIPTON

Curricula correlation

English National Curriculum

Spoken language	Give well-structured descriptions and explanations
Word reading	Apply their growing knowledge of root words, prefixes and suffixes (morphology and etymology), both to read aloud and to understand the meaning of new words that they meet
Comprehension	Discuss and evaluate how authors use language, including figurative language, considering the impact on the reader
	Draw inferences such as inferring characters, feelings, thoughts and motives from their actions, and justifying inferences with evidence
	Increase their familiarity with a wide range of books, including myths, legends and traditional stories, modern fiction, fiction from our literary heritage, and books from other cultures and traditions

Developing grammar, punctuation, vocabulary and spelling

Grammar and Punctuation	Dashes to indicate parenthesis	The four of us stood on the beach – yes, a beach! – and looked out in utter amazement. Then suddenly – BOOM! – a deafening explosion tore through the air as the gunpowder ignited.
Vocabulary and Spelling	Words containing the letter-string *ough*	thought, rough, although, through, enough
	Challenge and context words	unforgiving, ventured, experienced, conquer, necessary, underestimate, perseverance

Reading assessment points

Word reading	Can the children read a range of level appropriate texts fluently and accurately?
Comprehension	Can the children read between the lines, using clues from action, dialogue and description to interpret meaning and/or explain what characters are thinking/feeling and the way they act?
	Can the children identify the point of view from which a story is told and how this affects the reader's response (e.g. author's bias)?
	Can the children talk about the effects of different words and phrases to create different images and atmosphere?
	Can the children discuss messages, moods, feelings and attitudes using the clues from the text using inference and deduction skills?
	Can the children understand and explain different characters' points of view?
	Can the children quote directly from the text to answer questions?

Scottish Curriculum for Excellence

Listening and talking	I can select ideas and relevant information, organise these in an appropriate way for my purpose and use suitable vocabulary for my audience LIT 2-06a
Reading	I can select and use a range of strategies and resources before I read, and as I read, to make meaning clear and give reasons for my selection LIT 2-13a
	I can discuss the writer's style and other features appropriate to genre ENG 2-19a
	Through developing my knowledge of context clues, punctuation, grammar and layout, I can read unfamiliar texts with increasing fluency, understanding and expression ENG 2-12a
	To help me develop an informed view, I can identify and explain the difference between fact and opinion, recognise when I am being influenced, and have assessed how useful and believable my sources are LIT 2-18a

Welsh National Literacy Framework

Oracy	Explain information and ideas, exploring and using ways to be convincing, e.g. use of vocabulary, gesture, visual aids (Speaking)
Reading	Use a range of strategies to make meaning from words and sentences, including knowledge of phonics, word roots, word families, syntax, text organisation and prior knowledge of context (Reading strategies)
	Infer meaning which is not explicitly stated, e.g. what happens next?, why did he/she do that? (Comprehension)
	Identify and explore ideas and information that interest them (Comprehension)
	Identify how punctuation relates to sentence structure and how meaning is constructed in complex sentences (Reading strategies)

Northern Ireland Curriculum

Talking and Listening	Describe and talk about real experiences and imaginary situations and about people, places, events and artefacts
Reading	Use a range of cross-checking strategies to read unfamiliar words in texts
	Justify their responses logically, by inference, deduction and/or reference to evidence within the text, for example, compare and contrast two characters in a story or history text

Session 1 (Chapters 1–6)

About this book

This is an adaptation of Jules Verne's story of the same name which was originally published in 1864. It is a fantasy adventure story in which the characters find themselves in a variety of exciting situations and meet some unexpected dangers, such as dinosaurs.

You will need

- *What are they thinking, feeling, saying?* Photocopy Master, *Teaching Handbook* for Year 5/P6
- *Story planning frame* Photocopy Master, *Teaching Handbook* for Year 5/P6
- *Victorian inventions* Photocopy Master, *Teaching Handbook* for Year 5/P6

Before reading

- Discuss the title *Journey to the Centre of the Earth*. Have the children seen or heard of the film of the same name? What kind of narrative can we expect? **(activating prior knowledge, predicting)**
- Read the notes on page 2 to the children. Why would the girl Graüben have stayed at home in a Victorian story? **(inferring, engaging readers)**
- Remind the children what to do if they encounter a difficult word, or if they struggle to understand the meaning of a word or a sentence.

During reading

- Ask the children to read Chapters 1–6.
- As they read, ask them to look out for clues about the personalities of Axel, the Professor and Graüben.

Assessment point

Can the children read a range of level appropriate texts fluently and accurately?

After reading

Returning to the text

Ask the children:

- Where is Axel at the start of the story? **(inferring)**
- Referring to the text, how do you know that Axel is worried by the adventure? **(deducing, inferring and drawing conclusions, synthesizing)**
- How does Graüben feel about being left behind? **(empathizing)**

Assessment point

Can the children read between the lines, using clues from action, dialogue and description to interpret meaning and/or explain what characters are thinking/feeling and the way they act?

The author's craft

- Why does the author start his story near the end of the action with Axel writing his journal? How does this affect you as a reader? **(inferring, personal response)**
- How is the suspense built up at the end of Chapter 6? Has the reader been given enough clues to predict who the figure might be? **(synthesizing)**

Assessment point
Can the children identify the point of view from which a story is told and how this affects the reader's response (e.g. author's bias)?

Assessment point
Can the children talk about the effects of different words and phrases to create different images and atmosphere?

Developing comprehension

- Role play Chapters 3–5. Freeze frame the action at the point when the Professor says "*I can*" (p.9). Ask the children to show how their character is feeling, then ask them to say how they are feeling. **(personal response, adopting a critical response, empathizing)**
- Ask the children to complete the grid on the *What are they thinking, feeling, saying?* Photocopy Master for one of the characters at that point in the story. **(adopting a critical stance, empathizing)**

Assessment point
Can the children discuss messages, moods, feelings and attitudes using the clues from the text using inference and deduction skills?

Developing grammar, punctuation and spelling

- Write the words *thought*, *rough* and *although* on the board. Ask the children what these words have in common. Now ask them to say these words. Remind them that the letter group 'ough' can be pronounced in several different ways.

- Prior to Session 2, ensure the children have read Chapters 7–10 independently.

Session 2 (Chapters 11–15)

Before reading

- Ask the children to recap briefly the story so far. Did they guess who the hooded figure was? **(recall)**

During reading

- Ask the children to read Chapters 11–15.
- As they read, ask the children to look out for the author's use of dashes.
- Also ask them to look for evidence that Axel seems to be more worried than any other character. **(inferring and drawing conclusions)**

> **Assessment point**
> Can the children read a range of level appropriate texts fluently and accurately?

After reading

Returning to the text

Ask the children:

- What does the phrase *all grinning like schoolchildren* on page 25 say about how the characters were feeling? **(empathizing, inferring)**
- Where did the stream lead them to? **(recall)**

> **Assessment point**
> Can the children read between the lines, using clues from action, dialogue and description to interpret meaning and/or explain what characters are thinking/ feeling and the way they act?

The author's craft

- On page 33, the author writes about the fish, *It was a fascinating scientific discovery ... and soon a tasty meal!* What does this expression add to the creation of the scene? Can the children explain the humour and the contrast between the two parts of the sentence? How could they use this type of expression in their own writing?
- Focus on other expressions the author uses. Explain the use of the simile *as unbending as rock* (p.17). What insight does it give about Graüben's character?
- What expressions does the author use on page 21 to show how Axel is feeling as he looks down into the crater?

> **Assessment point**
> Can the children understand and explain different characters' points of view?

Developing grammar, punctuation and spelling

- Look at the examples the children have found of dashes in the text. Discuss how dashes are often used for parenthesis (to separate a word or phrase that has been added to a sentence as an explanation as an afterthought), e.g. *The four of us stood on the beach – yes, a beach! – and looked out in utter amazement* (p.30).
- Ask the children how the sentences could have been punctuated differently.

- Prior to Session 3, ensure the children have read Chapters 16–18 independently.

Session 3 (Chapters 19–24)

Before reading

- Ask the children to predict what will happen in the next few chapters. **(predicting)**

During reading

- Ask the children to read Chapters 19–24.
- As they read, ask them to mentally note how the characters managed to get back up to the earth's surface.

Assessment point
Can the children read a range of level appropriate texts fluently and accurately?

After reading

Returning to the text

- Ask the children to explain how the group returned to the earth's surface. **(recall)**

Assessment point
Can the children quote directly from the text to answer questions?

- Ask the children to discuss in pairs whether or not they think the narrative is believable and to support their views. **(synthesizing, personal response, adopting a critical stance)**

Developing comprehension

- Ask the children to think about the situations Axel was in. Draw an emotions graph to show the significant changes in Axel's emotions in the pages they have just read and discussed. **(empathizing, determining importance)**

Assessment point

Can the children read between the lines, using clues from action, dialogue and description to interpret meaning and/ or explain what characters are thinking/feeling and the way they act?

Developing vocabulary

- In pairs, ask the children to find words and phrases to describe the heat of the volcano on pages 57 and 58. How do they help the reader to visualize the scene? **(visualizing)**

Writing opportunity

- Ask the children to imagine that they have a laptop which works deep at the centre of the earth. Ask them to write a Twitter entry (maximum of 140 characters) for each day for a small part of the adventure.

Follow-up

Writing activities

- Write a short account, in the first person, of an adventure currently taking place in the news. **(short writing task)**
- Jules Verne wrote other adventure stories. Write a modern adventure story using all the technology we have available today. Use the *Story planning frame* Photocopy Master to help. **(longer writing task)**

Cross-curricular activities

- Turn the story into a play script and enact it. **(Drama)**
- Research volcanoes and their position in the world. Locate Sicily, Stromboli and Iceland. **(Geography)**
- Imagine you are organizing an expedition. Discuss the different types of personalities and skills it would be useful to have in your team. Are there some kinds of people who might be a burden on the expedition? **(PSHE)**

Beneath the Ice

BY MARTYN BEARDSLEY

Curricula correlation

English National Curriculum

Spoken language	Give well-structured descriptions and explanations
Word reading	Apply their growing knowledge of root words, prefixes and suffixes (morphology and etymology), both to read aloud and to understand the meaning of new words that they meet
Comprehension	Summarise the main ideas drawn from more than one paragraph, identifying key details that support the main ideas
	Continue to read and discuss an increasingly wide range of fiction, poetry, plays, non-fiction and reference books or textbooks
	Ask questions to improve their understanding
	Check that the book makes sense to them, discussing their understanding and exploring the meaning of words in context

Developing grammar, punctuation, vocabulary and spelling

Grammar and Punctuation	Verb prefixes *dis-*, *de-* and *re-*	discover, dishearten, defeated, depended, decided, described, retreated, returned, recovering, restore, reported
Vocabulary and Spelling	Endings which sound like /shun/, spelt *-tion*, *-sion*, *-ssion*	expedition, mission, conditions, invention, impression, combination, pollution, traditionally, location
	Challenge and context words	unforgiving, ventured, experienced, conquer, necessary, underestimate, perseverance

Reading assessment points

Word reading	Can the children read a range of level appropriate texts fluently and accurately?
Comprehension	Can the children compare and talk about the structures and features of a range of non-fiction texts?
	Can the children skim and scan to identify key ideas in the text?
	Can the children quote directly from the text to answer questions?
	Can the children refer to the text to support opinions and predictions?

Scottish Curriculum for Excellence

Listening and talking	I can select ideas and relevant information, organise these in an appropriate way for my purpose and use suitable vocabulary for my audience LIT 2-06a
Reading	I can select and use a range of strategies and resources before I read, and as I read, to make meaning clear and give reasons for my selection LIT 2-13a
	I can make notes, organise them under suitable headings and use them to understand information, develop my thinking, explore problems and create new texts, using my own words as appropriate LIT 2-15a
	I regularly select and read, listen to or watch texts which I enjoy and find interesting, and I can explain why I prefer certain texts and author LIT 2-11a
	To show my understanding, I can respond to literal, inferential and evaluative questions and other close reading tasks and can create different kinds of questions of my own ENG 2-17a

Welsh National Literacy Framework

Oracy	Explain information and ideas, exploring and using ways to be convincing, e.g. use of vocabulary, gesture, visual aids (Speaking)
Reading	Use a range of strategies to make meaning from words and sentences, including knowledge of phonics, word roots, word families, syntax, text organisation and prior knowledge of context (Reading strategies)
	Use a range of strategies for skimmming, e.g. finding key words, phrases, gist, main ideas, themes (Reading strategies)
	Identify and explore ideas and information that interest them (Comprehension)
	Gather and organise information and ideas from different sources (Response and analysis)

Northern Ireland Curriculum

Talking and Listening	Tell, retell and interpret stories based on memories, personal experiences, literature, imagination and the content of the curriculum
Reading	Use a range of cross-checking strategies to read unfamiliar words in texts
	Extend the range of their reading and develop their own preferences

Session 1 (pages 2–7)

About this book

Explorers have been searching for ways to cross the Arctic Ocean for thousands of years. This book highlights one adventurer – Sir John Franklin – and the extreme conditions he and his team had to face.

You will need

- Globe, atlases
- *Vocabulary word map* Photocopy Master, *Teaching Handbook* for Year 5/P6
- *Life in the Arctic* Photocopy Master, *Teaching Handbook* for Year 5/P6

Before reading

- Look at the front cover and discuss the title. What could be *Beneath the Ice*? Remind the children that the Arctic is frozen ice. **(predicting, activating prior knowledge)**
- Read pages 2–5 together. Discuss the maps and use a globe to help explain the North-West Passage. **(engaging readers)**
- Remind the children what to do if they encounter a difficult word, or if they struggle to understand the meaning of a word or a sentence.

During reading

- Ask the children to reread pages 2–5 and then to the end of page 7 independently.
- As they read, ask them to note words on the theme of ice and the cold.

Assessment point

Can the children read a range of level appropriate texts fluently and accurately?

After reading

Returning to the text

- Explain the difference between different question types: recall (answer is found easily in the text), inference (a clue to the answer is in the text) and synthesis. **(make connections, predict, draw conclusions)**
- In pairs, ask the children to devise one question of each type to ask the group about the sections they have just read. **(questioning)**

The author's craft

- Look at pages 2–3 and ask the children to identify the features of a recount text: orientation (scene-setting opening); events (recount of events as they occurred); reorientation (a closing statement with elaboration).

Assessment point
Can the children compare and talk about the structures and features of a range of non-fiction texts?

Developing comprehension

- Ask the children to comment on what they have read so far (content, features, layout, maps, etc). **(personal response)**

Developing vocabulary

- In pairs, ask the children to find and discuss the meaning and use of the themed vocabulary they identified earlier. Emphasize that details are needed in this genre to bring incidents alive.
- Complete the *Vocabulary word map* Photocopy Master.

Assessment point
Can the children skim and scan to identify key ideas in the text?

Session 2 (pages 8–17)

Before reading

- Ask the children to share any information they remember from Session 1. **(recall)**
- Quickly skim through pages 8–17 to get an overview of their contents. **(previewing the text)**

During reading

- Ask the children to read pages 8–17 independently, then go back and reread the sections that most interest them.
- Point out the word *expedition* on page 4. Ask the children to note other words that end with the /shun/ sound as they read.

- As they read, ask them to think about which sections they have found most interesting and why. They could make brief notes in their reading journals. **(personal response)**

Assessment point
Can the children read a range of level appropriate texts fluently and accurately?

After reading

Returning to the text

- Ask the children to talk about some of the sections/facts that interested them.
- Pair up the children who selected the same sections and ask them to devise questions for each other as they did in Session 1, taking turns to ask and answer the questions. **(questioning)**

Assessment point
Can the children quote directly from the text to answer questions?

The author's craft

- Look at 'How to make pemmican' on page 15. Identify the structural and language features of an instructional text (goal, materials, sequenced steps, use of imperative verbs).

Assessment point
Can the children compare and talk about the structures and features of a range of non-fiction texts?

Developing comprehension

- Ask the children to write a 'How to prepare for an expedition to the Arctic' instructional text using the survival facts on page 13.

Developing grammar, punctuation and spelling

- Look together at the words *impression* and *pollution*. Explain to the children that it can be difficult to know which ending to use.
- Remind children that if the root word ends *-t* or *-te* they should use *-tion*, if it ends *-d*, *-de* or *-se*, they should use *-sion*.

- Prior to Session 2, ensure the children have read pages 18–23 independently.

Session 3 (pages 24–30)

Before reading

- Ask the children to tell you any fact from their independent reading. **(recall)**

During reading

- Ask the children to read pages 24–30. They should be prepared to give an oral summary of one section.

Assessment point
Can the children read a range of level appropriate texts fluently and accurately?

After reading

Returning to the text

- Ask each child to give a brief oral summary of their chosen section. **(recall, summarizing, determining importance)**
- As they talk, model making brief summary notes, adding page numbers and key points.

Assessment point
Can the children refer to the text to support opinions and predictions?

The author's craft

- Read and discuss the letter on page 22. Identify the features of letter writing.

Developing comprehension

- In pairs, ask the children to make notes from the book in order to recount one of the expeditions or rescue missions described. Children should be prepared to retell the adventure using the notes, adding techniques such as exaggeration for effect and humour.

Developing grammar, punctuation and spelling

- Look at some of the words with verb prefixes in the book, e.g. *discover, returned*. Look together at the meaning the prefix has on the verb. Practise adding these prefixes to other words to see the effect they have.

Follow-up

Writing activities

- Ask the children to use their notes to develop an computer-based report on Arctic exploration, adding hyperlinks to visual material, e.g. maps. **(longer writing task)**
- In pairs, discuss a way to rescue Franklin, and write a letter outlining the idea. Use the letter on page 22 of *Beneath the Ice* as a model. **(short writing task)**
- Write a recipe for a favourite food to take on an expedition. **(short writing task)**

Further literacy activities

- Draw a timeline showing all the expeditions to search for the North-West Passage from the Vikings to the present day.

Cross-curricular activities

- Measure the maximum and minimum temperatures over a period of time and plot them on graphs. **(Science, Maths)**
- Compare and contrast desert and Arctic conditions and survival in each. **(Geography, Science)**
- Using the *Life in the Arctic* Photocopy Master, research how animals are adapted to the harsh conditions. **(Science)**
- Research icebreaker ships and explain their design and use. **(DT)**

Exploring the Deep

BY CHLOE RHODES

Curricula correlation

English National Curriculum

Spoken language	Ask relevant questions to extend their understanding and build vocabulary and knowledge
Word reading	Apply their growing knowledge of root words, prefixes and suffixes (morphology and etymology), both to read aloud and to understand the meaning of new words that they meet
Comprehension	Ask questions to improve their understanding
	Read books that are structured in different ways and reading for a range of purposes
	Identify how language, structure and presentation contribute to meaning
	Retrieve, record and present information from non-fiction

Developing grammar, punctuation, vocabulary and spelling

Grammar and Punctuation	Relative clauses beginning with *who, which, where, whose, that*	At night some parrot fish cover themselves in a clear coating of mucus, which masks their scent ... These are underwater mountain ranges that rise up from the ocean floor.
Vocabulary and Spelling	Words with endings sounding like /zhuh/ and /chuh/ (*-sure*/*-ture*)	measure, pressure, temperature, creature, mixture, features
	Challenge and context words	fearsome, communicate, decibels, microscopic, photosynthesis

Reading assessment points

Word reading	Can the children read a range of level appropriate texts fluently and accurately?
Comprehension	Can the children refer to the text to support opinions and elaborate?
	Can the children quote directly from the text to answer questions?
	Can the children compare and talk about the structures and features of a range of non-fiction texts?
	Can the children skim and scan to identify key ideas in the text?

Scottish Curriculum for Excellence

Listening and talking	I can show my understanding of what I listen to or watch by responding to literal, inferential, evaluative and other types of questions, and by asking different kinds of questions of my own LIT 2-07a
Reading	I can select and use a range of strategies and resources before I read, and as I read, to make meaning clear and give reasons for my selection LIT 2-13a
	To show my understanding, I can respond to literal, inferential and evaluative questions and other close reading tasks and can create different kinds of questions of my own ENG 2-17a
	Using what I know about the features of different types of texts, I can find, select and sort information from a variety of sources and use this for different purposes LIT 2-14a
	I can: discuss structure, characterisation and/or setting; discuss the writer's style and other features appropriate to genre ENG 2-19a

Welsh National Literacy Framework

Oracy	Listen to others, asking questions and responding to both the content and the speakers' viewpoints (Listening)
Reading	Use a range of strategies to make meaning from words and sentences, including knowledge of phonics, word roots, word families, syntax, text organisation and prior knowledge of context (Reading strategies)
	Identify features of texts, e.g. introduction to topic, sequence, illustrations, degree of formality (Reading strategies)
	Identify and explore ideas and information that interest them (Comprehension)
	Scan to find specific details using graphic and textual organisers, e.g. sub-headings, diagrams (Reading strategies)

Northern Ireland Curriculum

Talking and Listening	Share, respond to and evaluate ideas, arguments and points of view and use evidence or reason to justify opinions, actions or proposals
Reading	Use a range of cross-checking strategies to read unfamiliar words in texts
	Use traditional and digital sources to locate, select, evaluate and communicate information relevant for a particular task

Session 1 (pages 2–15)

What's beneath the waves? This book details what can be found deep in the oceans and how explorers and scientists have reached the depths.

You will need

- Globe, atlases
- *KWL* Photocopy Master, *Teaching Handbook* for Year 5/P6

Before reading

- Look at the front cover and discuss the title. Ask the children what they know about exploring the ocean and make brief notes on their *KWL* Photocopy Master under 'What I already know'. Looking at the contents page, and using the globe/atlases, ask them to work in pairs to discuss what they would like to know about oceans and seas. Make individual lists on the *KWL* sheet under 'What I would like to find out'. **(activating prior knowledge)**
- Read pages 2–5 together. Discuss the zones and make sure the children understand the differences in depth. **(engaging readers)**
- Remind the children what to do if they encounter a difficult word, or if they struggle to understand the meaning of a word or a sentence.

During reading

- Ask the children to read on to the end of page 15.
- Ask the children to refer to the glossary to help them understand some of the terms used, and to note down new, difficult or unknown words, e.g. *algae, photosynthesis*. Ask them to make a note of what they think they mean.
- As they read, ask them to mentally note any answers to the questions on their *KWL* sheet.

Assessment point
Can the children read a range of level appropriate texts fluently and accurately?

Assessment point
Can the children refer to the text to support opinions and elaborate?

After reading

Returning to the text

Ask the children:

- Discuss the differences between different question types: recall (answer is found easily in the text), inference (a clue to the answer is in the text) and synthesis (**make connections, predict, draw conclusions)**
- In pairs, ask the children to devise one question of each type about the sections they have just read to ask the group. **(questioning)**

Assessment point
Can the children quote directly from the text to answer questions?

The author's craft

- Look at the information cards on pages 6–7 and ask the children to identify the features of a non-chronological report: an opening title; a description of the phenomenon (including qualities, parts, habits, behaviour), third person, present tense.
- Ask them to write an information card about themselves and share it with others.

Assessment point
Can the children compare and talk about the structures and features of a range of non-fiction texts?

Developing vocabulary

- Ask them to share the vocabulary they noted and their meanings. Encourage them to check them with a dictionary.

Session 2 (pages 16–23)

Before reading

- Ask the children to share one piece of information they have added to their *KWL* sheet. **(recall)**

During reading

- Ask the children to read pages 16–23 independently, then to go back and reread the sections that most interest them.
- As they read, ask them to think about which sections they have found most interesting and why. **(personal response)**
- Ask the children to note any words ending with *-sure* or *-ture* as they read.

Assessment point
Can the children read a range of level appropriate texts fluently and accurately?

After reading

Returning to the text

- Ask the children to talk about some of the sections/facts that interested them.
- Pair up the children who selected the same sections and ask them to devise questions for each other, taking turns to ask and answer the questions. **(questioning)**

Assessment point
Can the children refer to the text to support opinions and elaborate?

Developing comprehension

- Ask the children to skim the book for animals, listing them under the various zones. (**summarizing**)

Assessment point
Can the children skim and scan to identify key ideas in the text?

Developing grammar, punctuation and spelling

- Ask the children to share the words they found with *-sure* and *-ture* endings. Using *pressure* and *temperature* (both p.16) as examples, explain how there is a slight difference in how these endings are pronounced. Words ending with the /zhuh/ sound are spelt *-sure* and those ending with the /chuh/ sound are spelt *-ture*.

Session 3 (pages 24–30)

Before reading

- Ask the children to tell you an interesting fact they have read. **(recall)**

During reading

- Ask the children to read pages 24–30. They should be prepared to give an oral summary of one section.

Assessment point

Can the children read a range of level appropriate texts fluently and accurately?

After reading

Returning to the text

Ask the children:

- What is the midnight zone? **(recall)**
- What is a hydrothermal vent? **(recall)**
- Why is Mauna Kea in Hawaii called the world's highest mountain?

Assessment point

Can the children quote directly from the text to answer questions?

Developing comprehension

- Ask the children to complete their *KWL* sheet and share their facts with a partner. **(summarizing, determining importance)**

Developing vocabulary

- Discuss the lists of vocabulary that the children collected during reading. Ask them to suggest which words would be useful to add to the glossary for a younger age group.

Developing grammar, punctuation and spelling

- Ask the children to look at the clause *which masks their scent* ... on page 6. Explain that this is a relative clause which gives additional information about the first clause and is connected to the main clause by a word such as *that, which, who, whom* or *whose*. Can they find any other relative clauses in the sections they have just read?

Follow-up

Writing activities

- Choose one zone and create an online information pack for holiday makers, e.g. what to see and how to see it. Work in pairs to create a series of digital pages that can be hyperlinked. **(longer writing task)**
- Research other famous shipwrecks and write information cards modelled on the ones on pages 10 and 11. **(short writing task)**
- Write a poem showing how it would feel and what someone would see whilst wearing a Jim Suit. **(short writing task)**

Cross-curricular activities

- Using the information on page 5 as a model, create a vertical axis which shows the highest mountain and the deepest trench. **(Maths, Geography)**
- Create a piece of music depicting a specific zone using tuned and untuned percussion. Record it. **(Music)**
- Find out and describe the life cycles of fish. **(Science)**